Contents

MW00799441

There's just something irresistible about wooden letters. Maybe it's the instant ____ The inviting surface just waiting for your creative touch, or the whimsical way t____ Wooden letters can be young, sweet, vintage chic, glitzy, and modern. You can ____ And whether it's for a kid's room or the kitchen, wooden letters let you create a ____ accent to personalize any room.

In this book, we decorate specific letters in specific sizes, but these techniques work with any letter of the alphabet—numbers too! And if you choose a different size, simply adjust the materials accordingly. Just get creative, express yourself, and have fun!

LEISURE ARTS, INC.
Little Rock, Arkansas

TWINE-WRAPPED WITH FLOWER

A twine-wrapped letter is naturally elegant, but wrapping the corners can be a challenge. Use this simple technique, and you'll be wrapping like a pro!

TIP
Choose a style of wooden letter with large enough openings to feed the twine through repeatedly.

Supplies:

6" wooden letter
1 spool of jute twine
9" x 12" forest green felt
1 blue button, ½"
fabric stiffening spray
 (like Beacon
 Adhesives™ Stiffen Stuff™)
tacky glue
hot glue & glue gun
clear tape
craft paintbrush
scissors
sandpaper
pencil

TWINE-WRAPPED  WITH FLOWER

1. Lightly sand the wooden letter.

2. Before you wrap the letter with twine, glue short twine strands onto the corners to cover them. To do this, cut several 3" strands of twine. (We used about 11 strands per corner.) Paint tacky glue on the corner. Lay the 3" strands side by side to cover the corner.

3. Crisscross the first layer by gluing 3" strands from front to back. Use this technique to cover all the corners. (Skip this step if you have a letter O. You chose the only letter with no corners!)

4. Cut a 5-yard length of twine, tape one end to the back of the wooden letter, and start wrapping the twine around the glued strands. Wrap a section with twine in one layer, then overlap with a second layer. When you reach the end of the twine length, tie on another 5-yard piece of twine, hiding the knot in the back. Continue wrapping.

5. If you have an area that is not covered due to a slant or curve in your letter, wrap another layer of twine in a different direction to cover. Use a little tacky glue if needed to hold the twine in place. Finish by tying the twine to itself in the back.

6. To make the flower, wrap the twine around your three middle fingers about 40 times. Slide the twine off your fingers, pinch in the center, and tie with a piece of twine. Spread the loops apart and shape into a flower. Spray with fabric stiffening spray until wet. Let dry.

7. To make the tendrils, wrap a 3" piece of twine around a pencil and tape the ends down. Spray with fabric stiffening spray. Let dry, then remove from the pencil. Repeat to make four tendrils.

8. Assemble the flower by cutting three leaf shapes from the felt. Hot glue them to the twine-covered letter. Hot glue the tendrils to the felt leaves, then add the flower. Cut a circle of felt slightly larger than the button. Top the flower with the circle of felt and finish with the button in the center.

YARN WITH ZIPPER ROSES

Dress up a wooden letter with stylish yarn and high fashion roses made from zippers!

TIP
This craft works great with papier-mâché letters, too!

Supplies:

7" wooden letter
1 skein of teal yarn
6" black zipper with metal teeth
10" white zipper with
 metal teeth
18" gray zipper with
 metal teeth
teal acrylic paint
tacky glue
hot glue & glue gun
clear tape
foam paintbrush
craft paintbrush
scissors
sandpaper
pencil

YARN WITH ZIPPER ROSES

1. Lightly sand the wooden letter. Using the foam paintbrush, paint the letter teal and let dry.

2. Before you start wrapping, glue short strands of yarn onto the corners to cover them. To do this, cut several 3" strands of yarn. Paint tacky glue on the corner. Lay the 3" strands side by side to cover the corner. (See detail photos on page 3.)

3. Crisscross the first layer by gluing 3" strands from front to back. Use this technique to cover all the corners.

4. Finish wrapping the letter by taping the end of a 5-yard piece of yarn to the back of the letter. Wrap the yarn around the glued strands. Wrap a section with yarn in one layer, then overlap with a second layer. When you reach the end of the yarn length, tie on another 5-yard piece of yarn, hiding the knot in the back. Continue wrapping.

5. If you have an area that is not covered due to a slant or curve in your letter, wrap another layer of yarn in a different direction to cover. Use a little tacky glue if needed to hold the yarn in place. Finish by tying the yarn to itself in the back.

6. To make each zipper rose, separate a zipper into two parts and use only one half. Run a 3" line of hot glue along the fabric edge of the zipper. Protecting your fingers, roll the zipper tightly around itself on the glue. Repeat until the whole zipper is glued and coiled. Push the center of the rose up higher than the sides to add dimension.

7. Hot glue the largest rose to the letter and nestle the other two roses in next to the first.

METALLIC EMBOSSED BUTTERFLIES

Take an unfinished letter from ordinary to extraordinary with copper flourishes and glittery embossed butterflies.

TIP
To make sure your stamp is fully inked, set the stamp face up on the table and press the ink pad onto the stamp.

Supplies:

7½" wooden letter
1 flourish stamp, 3"
1 butterfly stamp, 1½"
1 butterfly stamp, ¾"
1 dimensional butterfly sticker, 1½" x 2"
teal powdered fabric dye (like RIT®)
gold pigment ink stamp pad
copper pigment ink stamp pad
silver pigment ink stamp pad
gold embossing powder
multi-purpose heat gun
heat proof mixing cup
teaspoon
chopstick
drop cloth
protective gloves
craft paintbrush
foam paintbrush
sandpaper

METALLIC EMBOSSED BUTTERFLIES

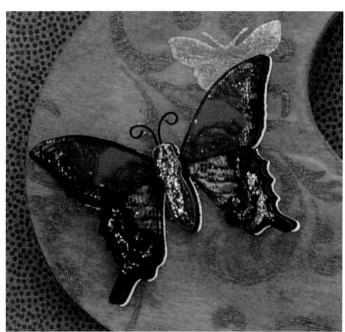

1. Lightly sand the wooden letter. To dye the letter, don your gloves and make a batch of teal dye by mixing ¾ cup steaming hot water with a teaspoon of dye. Stir with a chopstick. Over a drop cloth, use the foam paintbrush to paint the dye onto the letter. Let dry.

2. Using the copper ink and the flourish stamp, create a flourish pattern all over the surface of the letter, re-inking and rotating the stamp each time you use it. Let dry.

3. Stamp the small butterfly onto the letter using the gold ink. Immediately sprinkle the stamped ink with gold embossing powder. Repeat two more times, stamping the butterfly and dusting the ink with embossing powder immediately after each stamping.

4. Stamp the large butterfly onto the letter using the gold ink. Immediately sprinkle the stamped ink with gold embossing powder.

5. Let the powder and ink on the butterflies dry completely. When they are dry, shake off the excess embossing powder. Use a dry paintbrush to clean around the edges of the butterflies, removing any loose powder.

6. Hold the heat gun a few inches from the stamped butterfly image. Move the heat gun in a circular motion over the image just until the powder melts. Repeat for each stamped butterfly.

7. Stamp the small butterfly several times onto the letter using the silver ink, re-inking and rotating the stamp each time.

8. Adhere the dimensional butterfly sticker to the letter.

STENCILED FABRIC

Use stencils to get the look of a grain sack from a Paris flea market. Ooh la la!

Supplies:

13" wooden letter
½ yard natural Osnaburg fabric
 (or any similar linen or burlap)
½ yard fusible fleece
2 yards black piping trim, ¾" wide
2 yards red grosgrain ribbon, ¼" wide
3" x 3½" fleur-de-lis stencil
 (like Plaid® Decorative Icons)
1¼" x 1¼" flourish stencil
1" alphabet, number, and
 punctuation stencils
 (like Martha Stewart Crafts™
 Monogram Serif Stencil Set)
black acrylic paint
fabric glue
 (like Beacon Adhesives™
 Fabri-Tac™)
1¼" spouncer or stenciling
 sponge
iron & ironing board
pressing cloth
scissors
white chalk

STENCILED FABRIC

1. Prep the Osnaburg fabric by ironing out any wrinkles. Place the fusible fleece on the ironing board fusible side up and set the fabric on top. Dampen the pressing cloth and lay it on top of the fabric. With the iron on the wool/steam setting, press the cloth starting at the center. Press for 10 to 15 seconds in each area of the cloth until the entire piece of fabric is fused to the fleece. Let the fused fabric dry.

2. Set the wooden letter face up on the fabric, trace it with chalk, then set the letter aside. Arrange the stencils on the fabric so they are within or just overlapping the chalk outline.

3. Using the spouncer, dab small amounts of paint into the openings of the first stencil with a straight up and down motion. Be careful not to get paint underneath the edges of the stencil. Let dry. Use this technique to paint the rest of the stencils and let dry.

4. Cut the letter out leaving a ½" border outside the chalk line. Glue the fabric letter to the front of the wooden letter by spreading fabric glue onto the surface of the wooden letter. Wrap and glue the edges of the fabric down around the sides of the wooden letter.

5. Cover the sides of the letter by gluing the flat side of the piping trim around the edge, starting at the bottom of the letter. If the piping trim is too wide, trim it flush with the back of the letter. Glue the red ribbon over the flat side of the piping trim.

DECOUPAGED WITH BEADED KEY

Create a vintage monogram with sheet music, an old key, and a tape measure straight from grandma's sewing box!

TIP

Wrinkles that appear when decoupaging paper to wood will usually disappear when the paper dries.

Supplies:

9" wooden letter
1 sheet heirloom sheet
 music scrapbook paper
1 sheet teal scrapbook paper
1 sheet aqua & teal flourish
 scrapbook paper
1 metal key, 2"
 (like Tim Holtz™
 Idea-ology™ Word Keys)
1 heart-shaped padlock
 charm
1 red jeweled brad
4 blue faceted beads, 3mm
2 clear faceted beads, 6mm
9" red satin ribbon, ⅛" wide
1 red tape measure
20-gauge copper wire
decoupage medium
 (like Mod Podge®)
clear spray paint
hot glue & glue gun
craft paintbrush
wire snips
pinking shears or
 decorative-edged scissors
scissors
sandpaper
pencil

DECOUPAGED WITH BEADED KEY

1. Lightly sand the wooden letter. To prevent the sheet music scrapbook paper from buckling, spray both sides with a light coat of clear spray paint and let dry. Trace the wooden letter onto the sheet music, then cut it out and glue it to the wooden letter using decoupage medium. Once dry, paint a coat of decoupage medium over the surface of the paper and let dry.

2. Starting at the bottom of the wooden letter, hot glue the tape measure all the way around the outside edge of the letter and trim the end.

3. Wrap the copper wire around a section of the letter approximately 25 times. Twist the wire around itself in the back to secure and trim the end with wire snips.

4. Wrap the shaft of the key with copper wire, sliding on a bead or two with each wrap. Twist the end of the wire around itself in the back. Using the red ribbon, tie the key and the padlock charm to the wire wrap on the letter.

5. To make the pleated rosette, cut two 1" x 12" strips of solid teal scrapbook paper. Accordion pleat the strips by folding the paper back and forth. Glue the ends of the strips together to make one long strip. Fan the strip into a rosette and glue the remaining ends together. Dab a little hot glue on the back to maintain the rosette shape.

6. Cut a 1" circle out of the flourish scrapbook paper using pinking shears. Poke the jeweled brad through the center of the circle and into the center of the pleated rosette and secure with a little hot glue. Hot glue the rosette to the letter.

CRACKLE PAINT / MIXED MEDIA

Turn a plain letter into a shabby chic delight with patterned paper,
beaded trims, and fancy flowers!

TIP
This letter is fun to personalize and make your own. So start in the scrapbook paper aisle, choose some patterns you love, then go wild with embellishments.

Supplies:

10½" wooden letter
3 sheets coordinating scrapbook papers
6" glittered green leaf border sticker
 (like Recollections™ Glitter On A Roll™)
6" beaded lace trim, ¾" wide
13" coral satin ribbon, ³/₈" wide
3 magenta silk flowers, 1½" to 2"
3 rhinestone shank buttons, ½"
16 self-adhesive half-pearls, ¼"
water-based wood stain
 (like Maple FolkArt® Stain)
white acrylic paint
decoupage medium
 (like Mod Podge®)
tacky glue
hot glue & glue gun
foam paintbrush
masking tape
scissors
sandpaper
pencil

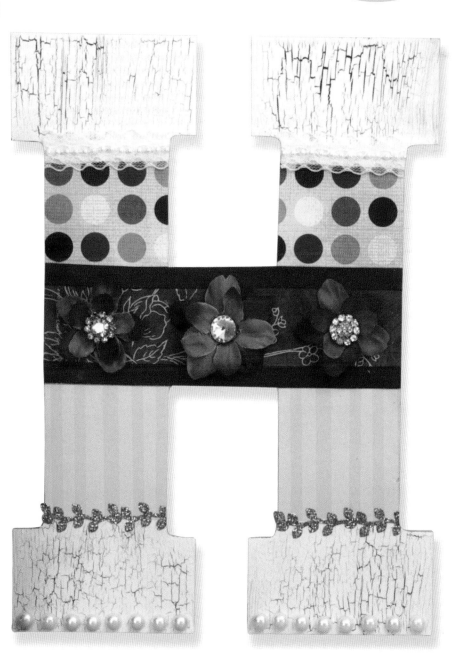

CRACKLE PAINT / MIXED MEDIA

1. Lightly sand the wooden letter. Section off the top and bottom areas to be crackle painted using the masking tape. Apply a coat of wood stain using a foam paintbrush and let dry. Paint a thick layer of tacky glue over the stained wood, and let the glue dry just until it forms a film on top. Paint over the glue with white paint and let dry. The white paint will crackle as the paint and glue dry. Remove the tape.

2. Trace and cut a piece of scrapbook paper to fit your letter next to the crackled paint at the top. Glue in place using decoupage medium. Cut a different piece of scrapbook paper to cover the area above the bottom crackled paint and glue into place. Finally, trace and cut a piece of the last scrapbook paper to cover the remaining exposed area of the letter and glue into place.

3. Cover the top seam between the paper and crackled paint with the beaded trim and hot glue. Layer the ribbon over the seams at the center of the letter. Then cover the bottom seam with the green leaf border sticker.

4. Remove a flower from its stem and hot glue it to the center of the letter. Repeat to add a flower to either side of the first. Top the flowers with rhinestone buttons.

5. Embellish the bottom edge of the letter with a row of self-adhesive half-pearls.

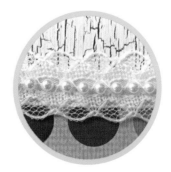

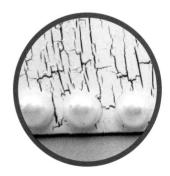

GLITTERED FOAM FLOWERS

Brighten up a girl's room with a sparkly initial covered in flowers galore!

TIP

Make a stellar letter for a boy's room using stars instead of flowers!

Supplies:

12" wooden letter
45 self-adhesive glittered craft foam flowers, 1" to 2"
45 self-adhesive craft foam shapes, ¼" to 1"
28 self-adhesive glitter flower stickers, ¾"
10 flower-shaped rhinestones, ½"
Cayman Blue FolkArt® Acrylic Paint
Turquoise FolkArt® Extreme Glitter™ Paint
tacky glue
foam paintbrush
sandpaper

GLITTERED FOAM FLOWERS

1. Lightly sand the wooden letter. Paint the letter with the Cayman Blue paint using the foam paintbrush. Let dry, then paint with the Turquoise Glitter Paint. Let dry.

2. Arrange a layer of the largest craft foam flowers on the surface of the letter. Peel and stick each one into place. Add a second layer of small, medium, and large flowers and craft foam shapes on top of the first layer, overlapping the flowers below. Fill in the gaps between shapes with smaller shapes until the letter is covered.

3. Adhere glittered stickers to the centers of the flowers on the top layer. Glue flower rhinestones to the centers of some of the flowers.

EMBELLISHED SHELLS

Applying a gold leaf finish is easier than you think, and it looks like a million bucks! Top it with gems from the sea and your letter will be a real treasure.

TIP
If the gold leaf isn't sticking to the letter in a few spots, don't worry. You can add a little more adhesive sizing, then apply more gold leaf when the adhesive becomes tacky.

Supplies:

7" wooden letter
4 gold leaf sheets, $5\frac{1}{2}$" x $5\frac{1}{2}$"
60 medium shells,
 $\frac{3}{4}$" to $1\frac{1}{4}$"
20 small shells,
 $\frac{1}{4}$" to $\frac{1}{2}$"
5 crystal AB rhinestones,
 5mm
9 crystal AB rhinestones, 4mm
14 pearls, 6mm
fine iridescent glitter
metal leaf adhesive sizing
clear acrylic sealer
hot glue & glue gun
foam paintbrush
craft paintbrush
sandpaper

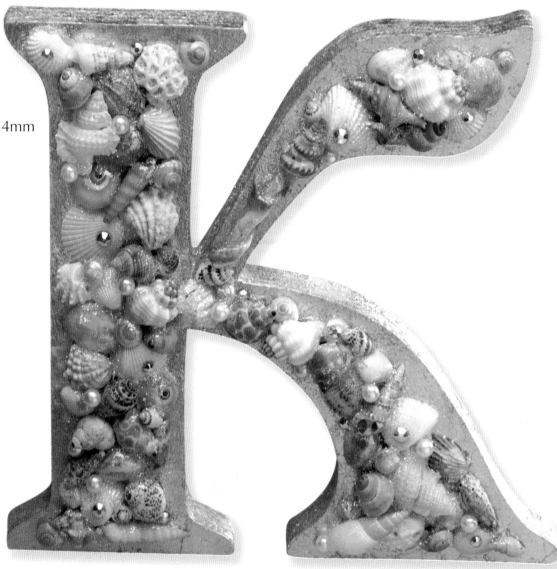

EMBELLISHED SHELLS

1. Lightly sand the wooden letter. Apply two coats of clear acrylic sealer to the front and sides of the letter using the foam paintbrush. Let dry between coats.

2. Apply a coat of metal leaf adhesive sizing using a craft paintbrush. Let dry. Apply a second coat and let dry until tacky.

3. Lay a sheet of gold leaf on the sticky surface of the letter, smoothing out any wrinkles with your finger. Continue adding more gold leaf until the front and sides of the letter are covered. Use a dry craft paintbrush to brush off any excess metal leaf pieces. (You can save these for your next project!)

4. Paint the gold-leafed surface with clear acrylic sealer using a foam paintbrush and let dry.

5. Arrange a layer of medium shells flat on the front of the letter, leaving a 1/8" border of gold leaf showing. Hot glue each shell into place. Fill in the gaps with the small shells.

6. To make the shells sparkle, apply small amounts of clear acrylic sealer between the shells, then dust with iridescent glitter. Work on one area at a time, as the clear acrylic sealer dries quickly. Use a dry paintbrush to brush the excess glitter off the tops of the shells.

7. Finish by hot gluing rhinestones here and there, then gluing pearls into the spaces between the shells.

General Painting Supplies

Lists of specific materials, acrylic paint colors, and paintbrushes used to complete the letters and projects are included with the instructions. Follow manufacturer's instructions to use the products in this book. Use spray sealer, primer, and paint in a well-ventilated area.

Wooden letters
Acrylic paints
Paintbrushes
Sandpaper
Tack cloth
Wood sealer
White spray primer
Tracing paper
Transfer paper
Stylus
Varnish
Painter's masking tape
Ruler
Craft glue
Hot glue gun
Assorted ribbons

General Instructions

Preparing the Letters

Sand the letter and wipe the sanding dust away with the tack cloth. Apply sealer to the letter and allow it to dry. Lightly sand the letter and wipe away the dust again. Apply primer to the letter; allow the primer to dry.

Patterns

The flowers in this book were painted in a freehand style without the use of a pattern. If you feel more comfortable using a pattern, follow the instructions below and use the patterns with the projects to transfer the flower outlines to your letter.

Trace the pattern onto tracing paper. Position the tracing paper on the letter as desired. Slide a piece of transfer paper between the traced pattern and the letter. Use a dull pencil or stylus to trace over the pattern lines.

Mixing Ratios

When following a mixing ratio, the first number refers to the number of parts of the first color listed and the second number refers to the number of parts of the second color listed. Mix the colors as directed by the ratio. Use an equal measurement, such as one drop, to measure one part.

Basecoating

Basecoating creates total opaque (solid) paint coverage. Use the largest Flat Shader brush with which you are comfortable. Load the brush with paint and evenly apply a thin, solid coat of paint. Begin in the center of the area to be basecoated and work your way out to the edge of the area. This will prevent brushstroke ridges from forming in the wet paint. If ridges do form, lightly brush over them before the paint dries. Repeat to add additional coats of paint as necessary.

Double-loading

Load a Flat Shader brush with the first color listed. Pull one corner of the brush through the second, contrasting color listed. Stroke the brush back and forth on the palette several times to blend the paint colors into the brush. There should be an even blending of the colors across the brush. Refer to the project photography and instructions for color placement and paint. Stop, rinse, and reload the brush when the contrasting color travels over to the opposite side of the brush.

Finishing the Letters

Apply two to three coats of varnish to the letter, allowing the varnish to dry between each application.

¾" FOAM

SCRUFFY BRUSH

#4 FILBERT

#6 FILBERT

#10/0 LINER

#5 ROUND

#4 FLAT SHADER

#6 FLAT SHADER

#8 FLAT SHADER

BLACK-EYED SUSAN

1 TITANIUM WHITE

2 LEMON YELLOW

3 PRIMARY YELLOW

4 TANGERINE

5 DEEP ORANGE

6 HONEY BROWN

7 BURNT UMBER

8 DARK CHOCOLATE

Palette:

Paintbrushes:
#6 Filbert
#10/0 Liner
Scruffy Brush
#5 Round Brush
#6 Flat Shader

Read the General Instructions on page 19 before beginning to paint. Unless otherwise indicated, allow the paint to dry after each application.

1. Basecoat the letter with Lemon Yellow.
2. Double-load a #6 Filbert with Primary Yellow and Tangerine. Paint the flower petals.
3. Thin Deep Orange with water to an ink-like consistency. Use a #10/0 Liner to paint the lines on the flower petals.
4. Use a Scruffy Brush to pounce the flower centers with Honey Brown; do not allow the paint to dry. Pounce the shading on the flower centers with Burnt Umber.
5. Thin Dark Chocolate with water to an ink-like consistency. Use the tip of a #5 Round Brush to paint the dots on the flower centers.
6. Use a #6 Flat Shader to paint the stripes on the sides of the letter with Titanium White.

WOODEN FRAME   CANVAS ALBUM

Supplies:
6¹/₂" x 8¹/₂" wooden frame
Cardboard
Coordinating scrapbook paper
Palette and Paintbrushes listed on page 20
General Supplies listed on page 18

Read the General Instructions on page 19 before beginning to paint. Unless otherwise indicated, allow the paint to dry after each application.

1. Basecoat the frame with Lemon Yellow.
2. Follow the **Black-Eyed Susan** instructions on page 20 to paint the flowers on the frame.
3. Basecoat the letter with Burnt Umber.
4. Cut a piece of cardboard to fit in the frame. Wrap and use craft glue to cover the cardboard piece with scrapbook paper. Insert the covered cardboard in the frame.
5. Use craft glue to glue the letter inside the frame. Glue ribbon around the frame.
6. Tie a length of ribbon into a bow. Hot glue the bow to the frame.

Supplies:
9⁵/₈" x 11¹/₂" canvas album
1" dia. button
Palette and Paintbrushes listed on page 20
General Supplies listed on page 18

Read the General Instructions on page 19 before beginning to paint. Unless otherwise indicated, allow the paint to dry after each application.

1. Follow the **Black-Eyed Susan** instructions on page 20 to paint the letter.
2. Use craft glue to glue the letter and ribbon border to the album.
3. Hot glue the bow and button to the album.

MARIGOLD

Palette:

1 TITANIUM WHITE

2 PINEAPPLE

3 PRIMARY YELLOW

4 PEACHY CREAM

5 BRIGHT ORANGE

6 CADMIUM ORANGE

7 TRUE RED

Paintbrushes:
#6 Filbert
#4 and #6 Flat Shaders
Scruffy Brush

Read the General Instructions on page 19 before beginning to paint. Allow the paint to dry after each application.

1. Basecoat the letter with Peachy Cream.
2. Double-load a #6 Filbert with Cadmium Orange and Bright Orange. Paint the outer flower petals on the orange marigolds.
3. Double-load a #4 Flat Shader with Pineapple and Primary Yellow. Paint the inner flower petals on the orange marigolds.
4. Use a Scruffy Brush to pounce the orange marigold flower centers with Bright Orange, True Red, and Pineapple.
5. Double-load a #6 Filbert with True Red and Cadmium Orange. Paint the outer flower petals on the red marigolds.
6. Double-load a #4 Flat Shader with Bright Orange and Primary Yellow. Paint the inner flower petals on the red marigolds.
7. Use a Scruffy Brush to pounce the red marigold flower centers with Bright Orange, True Red, and Pineapple.
8. Use a #6 Flat Shader to paint the stripes on the sides of the letter with Titanium White.

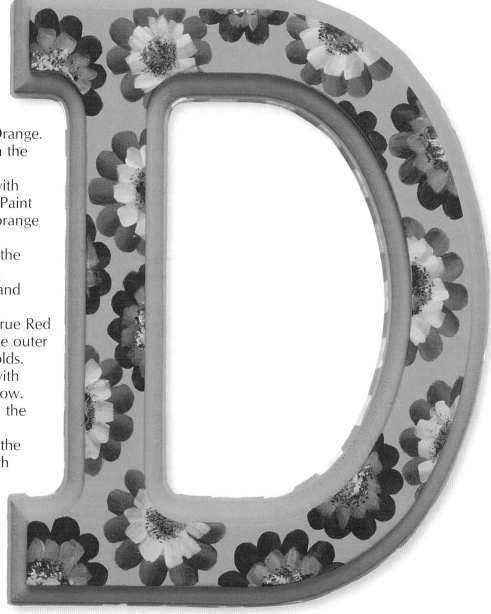

WOODEN PLAQUE GALVANIZED TUB

Supplies:
6³/₄" x 9¹/₂" wooden plaque with routed edges
Household sponge
Palette and Paintbrushes listed on page 22
General Supplies listed on page 18

Read the General Instructions on page 19 before beginning to paint. Allow the paint to dry after each application.

1. Basecoat the plaque with Peachy Cream.
2. Mask off the center of the plaque. Sponge paint the edges of the plaque with Cadmium Orange and Bright Orange. Remove the masking tape after the paint is dry.
3. Follow the **Marigold** instructions on page 22 to paint the flowers around the center of the plaque, leaving room at the center for the letter.
4. Basecoat the letter with True Red.
5. Sponge paint the top of the letter with Bright Orange and Primary Yellow.
6. Use craft glue to glue the letter, ribbon border, and ribbon hanger to the plaque.

Supplies:
16" x 9¹/₄" galvanized tub
Krylon® Bright Idea Yellow spray paint
³/₄" dia. foam brush
Bright Orange acrylic paint
Palette and Paintbrushes listed on page 22
General Supplies listed on page 18

Read the General Instructions on page 19 before beginning to paint. Allow the primer and paint to dry after each application.

1. Follow the **Marigold** instructions on page 22 to paint the letter.
2. Mask off the edges and inside of the tub. Apply primer to the tub. Spray paint the tub. Remove the masking tape after the paint is dry.
3. Use the foam brush to paint dots on the tub with Cadium Orange.
4. Hot glue ribbons around the rim and the letter to the tub.

DOGWOOD

Palette:

1
TITANIUM
WHITE

2
CARIBBEAN
BLUE

3
EGGSHELL

4
LIGHT
CINNAMON

5
CHARCOAL
GREY

Paintbrushes:
#4 Filbert
#10/0 Liner
Scruffy Brush
#0 Script Liner
#6 Flat Shader

Read the General Instructions on page 19 before beginning to paint. Unless otherwise indicated, allow the paint to dry after each application.

1. Basecoat the letter with Caribbean Blue + Titanium White (1:1).
2. Use a #4 Filbert to paint the flower petals with Titanium White. (This will require three coats of paint for full coverage.)
3. Double-load a #4 Filbert with Titanium White and Eggshell. Paint the shading and the indentions at the tips of the flower petals.
4. Thin Light Cinnamon with water to an ink-like consistency. Use a #10/0 Liner to paint the lines on the flower petals.
5. Use a Scruffy Brush to pounce the flower centers with Light Cinnamon. While the paint is still wet, pounce the highlights on the flower centers with Eggshell and the shading on the flower centers with Charcoal Grey.
6. Thin Charcoal Grey with water to an ink-like consistency. Use a #0 Script Liner to paint the branches, rolling and turning the brush between your index finger and thumb as you paint.
7. Use a #6 Flat Shader to paint the stripes on the sides of the letter with Titanium White.

BLUE CANVAS KEEPSAKE BOX

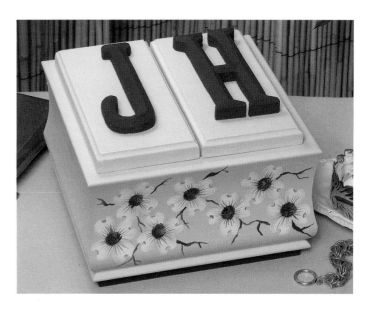

Supplies:
8" x 10" pre-primed artist canvas
Palette and Paintbrushes listed on page 24
General Supplies listed on page 18

Read the General Instructions on page 19 before beginning to paint. Unless otherwise indicated, allow the paint to dry after each application.

1. Follow the **Dogwood** instructions on page 24 to paint the letter.
2. Mask off a 6¼" x 8¼" area at the center of the canvas. Basecoat the edges of the canvas with Charcoal Grey + Light Cinnamon (1:1). Remove the masking tape after the paint is dry.
3. Use craft glue to glue the letter and the ribbon border to the canvas.

Supplies:
6³/₈" x 4" wooden keepsake box
Palette and Paintbrushes listed on page 24
General Supplies listed on page 18

Read the General Instructions on page 19 before beginning to paint. Unless otherwise indicated, allow the paint to dry after each application.

1. Basecoat the box with Caribbean Blue + Titanium White (1:1). Basecoat the base of the box and the letters with Charcoal Grey + Light Cinnamon (1:1).
2. Follow the **Dogwood** instructions on page 24 to paint the flowers on the front of the box.
   Use craft glue to glue the letters to the box.

FORGET-ME-NOT

Palette:

 1 TITANIUM WHITE
 2 CADMIUM YELLOW
 **3** CARIBBEAN BLUE
 4 BABY BLUE
 5 MEDIUM BLUE
 6 MINT GREEN
 7 OLIVE GREEN
 8 MEDIUM GREEN

Paintbrushes:
#4 and #6 Filberts
#10/0 Liner
#5 Round Brush
#6 Flat Shader

Read the General Instructions on page 19 before beginning to paint. Allow the paint to dry after each application.

1. Basecoat the letter with Mint Green + Titanium White (1:1).
2. Use a #6 Filbert to paint the flower petals with Caribbean Blue.
3. Use a #4 Filbert to paint the flower centers with Baby Blue.
4. Use a #10/0 Liner to paint the lines on the flower centers with Medium Blue.
5. Use the tip of a #5 Round Brush to paint the dots at the flower centers with Titanium White and Cadmium Yellow.
6. Double-load a #6 Flat Shader with Olive Green and Medium Green. Paint the leaves.
7. Use a #6 Flat Shader to paint the stripes on the sides of the letter with Titanium White.

OVAL CANVAS LINED BASKET

Supplies:
8" x 10" oval pre-primed artist canvas
#8 Filbert
#10 Flat Shader
Palette and Paintbrushes listed on page 26
General Supplies listed on page 18

Read the General Instructions on page 19 before beginning to paint. Allow the paint to dry after each application.

1. Basecoat the canvas with Mint Green + Titanium White (1:1).
2. Using a #8 Filbert to paint the flower petals, a #6 Filbert to paint the flower centers, and a #10 Flat Shader to paint the stripes, follow the Forget-Me-Not instructions on page 26 to paint the flowers on the center and the stripes around the edge of the canvas. Add Titanium White dots around the flowers.
3. Basecoat the letter with Titanium White.
4. Use craft glue to glue the letter to the center of the canvas and the ribbon around the canvas.

Supplies:
10¹/₂" x 12" lined basket
Palette and Paintbrushes listed on page 26
General Supplies listed on page 18

Read the General Instructions on page 19 before beginning to paint. Allow the paint to dry after each application.

1. Follow the Forget-Me-Not instructions on page 26 to paint the letter.
2. Hot glue the letter to the basket.

ROSE

Palette:

 1 TITANIUM WHITE

 2 HYDRANGEA PINK

 3 PEONY PINK

 4 CRIMSON

 5 LIGHT AVOCADO

 6 LIGHT GREEN

Paintbrushes:
#4, #6, and #8 Flat Shaders

Read the General Instructions on page 19 before beginning to paint. Allow the paint to dry after each application.

1. Basecoat the letter with Hydrangea Pink.
2. For pink roses, double-load a #8 Flat Shader with Peony Pink and Titanium White. Paint the petal at the top of each rose. Now, paint the petals at the base of each rose.
3. For red roses, double-load a #8 Flat Shader with Crimson and Titanium White. Paint the petal at the top of each rose. Now, paint the petals at the base of each rose.
4. Double-load a #4 Flat Shader with Light Green and Light Avocado. Paint the leaves.
5. Use a #6 Flat Shader to paint the stripes on the sides of the letter with Titanium White.

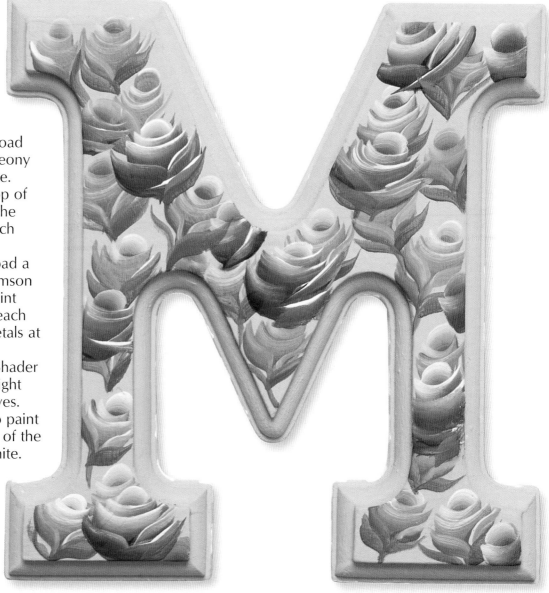

ROSE CANVAS   ROSE MONOGRAM

Supplies:
8" square pre-primed artist canvas
Palette and Paintbrushes listed on page 28
General Supplies listed on page 18

Read the General Instructions on page 19 before beginning to paint. Allow the paint to dry after each application.

1. Mask off a 6¹/₂" square area at the center of the canvas. Basecoat the center of the canvas with Hydrangea Pink.
2. Follow the **Rose** instructions on page 28 to paint the flowers on the center of the canvas. Remove the masking tape after the paint is dry.
3. Basecoat the letter with Light Green.
4. Use craft glue to glue the letter and the ribbon border to the canvas.

Supplies:
Wooden letter
Palette and Paintbrushes
listed on page 28
General Supplies listed
on page 18
Read the General Instructions on page 19 before beginning to paint. Allow the paint to dry after each application.

1. Follow the **Rose** instructions on page 28 to paint the flowers on the front of the letter and the stripes on the sides.

HYDRANGEA

Palette:

1 TITANIUM WHITE

2 FRENCH VANILLA

3 WISTERIA

4 SAPPHIRE

5 LAVENDER

6 GRAPE

Paintbrushes:

#4 Filbert
#5 Round Brush
#6 Flat Shader

Read the General Instructions on page 19 before beginning to paint. Unless otherwise indicated, allow the paint to dry after each application.

1. Basecoat the letter with Wisteria.

2. Paint a small area on the letter with Lavender. While the paint is still wet, use a #4 Filbert to paint the flower petals with Titanium White.

3. Paint another small area on the letter with Sapphire. While the paint is still wet, use a #4 Filbert to paint the flower petals with Titanium White.

4. Paint another small area on the letter with Grape. While the paint is still wet, use a #4 Filbert to paint the flower petals with Titanium White.

5. Repeat Steps 2-4 until the letter is covered with flowers, reloading the #4 Filbert with white paint often as you paint the flowers.

6. Use the tip of a #5 Round Brush to paint the dots at the flower centers with French Vanilla.

7. Use a #6 Flat Shader to paint the stripes on the sides of the letter with Titanium White.

WELCOME BASKET WALL BASKET

Supplies:
20¹/₄" x 10" pre-primed artist canvas
#6 Filbert
Black fine-point permanent marker
Palette and Paintbrushes listed on page 30
General Supplies listed on page 18

*Read the General Instructions on page 19
before beginning to paint. Unless otherwise
indicated, allow the paint to dry after each
application.*

1. Mask off a 16¹/₈" x 6" area at the center of the
   canvas. Working on one small section at a time
   and using a #6 Filbert to paint the petals, follow
   the **Hydrangea** instructions on page 30 to
   paint the edges of the canvas. Remove the
   masking tape after the paint is dry.
2. Use the ruler and marker to draw a line along the
   edge of the painted area on the canvas.
3. Basecoat the letters with Wisteria.
4. Use craft glue to glue the letters to the center of
   the canvas.

Supplies:
12" x 13¹/₂" hanging wall
  basket
Palette and Paintbrushes
  listed on page 30
General Supplies listed on
  page 18

*Read the General Instructions on page 19 before
beginning to paint. Unless otherwise indicated, allow
the paint to dry after each application.*

1. Follow the **Hydrangea** instructions on
   page 30 to paint the letter.
2. Hot glue the ribbon, bow, letter, and hanger to
   the basket.

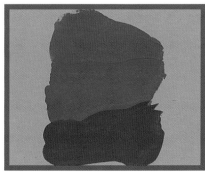

CREDITS

GRAPHIC DESIGNER

Kathleen Young

We have made every effort to ensure that these instructions are accurate and complete. We cannot, however, be responsible for human error, typographical mistakes, or variations in individual work.

PROJECTS FEATURED ON PAGES 20–31 DESIGNED BY

Patti Wallenfang

LEISURE ARTS
the art of everyday living
www.leisurearts.com

CRAFT PROJECTS ON PAGES 2–17 DESIGNED BY

Jennifer & Kitty O'Neil
www.ONeilSisters.com

PRODUCTION MANAGER

Bob Humphrey